IMAGES
of America

USCG AIR STATION
AND GROUP ASTORIA

The Astoria-Megler Bridge, approximately 10 miles from the Pacific Ocean, links Oregon on the left to Washington on the right. (Author's collection.)

An HH-52 helicopter hoists a crewman from a 44-foot Coast Guard motor lifeboat. (US Coast Guard.)

IMAGES
of America

USCG AIR STATION AND GROUP ASTORIA

Susan L. Glen

ARCADIA
PUBLISHING

Published by Arcadia Publishing
Charleston, South Carolina

Printed in the United States of America

Library of Congress Control Number: 2011934317

For all general information, please contact Arcadia Publishing:
Telephone 843-853-2070
Fax 843-853-0044
E-mail sales@arcadiapublishing.com
For customer service and orders:
Toll-Free 1-888-313-2665

Visit us on the Internet at www.arcadiapublishing.com

This book is dedicated to the men and women of the US Coast Guard who serve and have served at Coast Guard Group and Air Station Astoria and especially to those who have given their lives in the performance of their duties.

CONTENTS

ACKNOWLEDGMENTS

Great appreciation for assistance with information or photographs for this book goes to: Rear Adm. Edward Nelson, USCG (Ret.); Capt. Jeffrey Hartman, USCG (Ret.); Cdr. John Glen, USCG (Ret.); Public Affairs Office Sector Columbia; Cdr. Bernie Hoyland, USCG (Ret.); Capt. Robert Ginn, USCG (Ret.); CPO John Furqueron, USCG (Ret.); CPO Herbert L. Goodland, USCG (Ret.); CWO4 Donald L. Nolan, USCG (Ret.); SCPO Jim Sherman, USCG (Ret.); and MCPO Darell Gelakoska and Mrs. James Maher.

The original crew of the air station when it opened are called "Plank Owners." They include Cdr. Robert L. Lawless, LCDR Robert C. Branham, LCDR Robert R. Houvener, Lt. Richard L. Burns, Lt. Brinton R. Shannon, Lt. John M. Wypick, W3 Robert G. Keim, W2 Ernest C. Moore III, AD1 George M. Baron, SA Daniel R. Belknap, ADC Kenneth R. Berlin, ATC Floyd L. Booren Jr., ET3 Robert P. Borger, AE3 Earl Brannon, AT2 Charles D. Crewse, AT3 Marion E. Dennison, AD2 Donald A. Falls, AM2 Herbert L. Goodland, SK1 Worth H. Hopkins, YN2 Ronald G. Humphrey, AT3 Warren L. Jones, AE1 Roger O. Lake, PR2 Louie A. Levy, AE2 Jack D. Meyers, AD3 Dale A. Perkins, AM1 Edward R. Pritchett, AT1 Ernie C. Rackley, AD2 James R. Serbin, and ET3 James D. Twogood.

INTRODUCTION

Coast Guard Group/Air Station Astoria is located at the Warrenton-Astoria Regional Airport on Young's Bay, adjacent to the Columbia River in Warrenton, Oregon. The missions of this military facility include search and rescue, homeland security, enforcement of laws and treaties, pollution response, and maintenance of over 500 aids to navigation.

The area of operations includes over 140 miles of coastline from Queets, Washington (to the north), to Pacific City, Oregon (to the south). Helicopters from Air Station Astoria patrol and respond to offshore missions from the Canadian border to the California border. Along with the helicopters, motor lifeboat stations at Cape Disappointment, Tillamook Bay, and Grays Harbor are continually on alert. In 1966, two Bell HH-13N helicopters were also deployed from Air Station Astoria to the new USCG icebreaker *Northwind* on patrol in the Arctic.

The Group provides supply, administration, medical care, naval and civil engineering, communications, and other support to all of its units, as well as some support to the buoy tender located at Tongue Point. Additional support is also provided to the Electronic Support Detachment, Marine Safety Detachment, Aids to Navigation Team, National Motor Lifeboat School, and the Advanced Rescue Swimmer School. Two Pacific-area Coast Guard cutters were also given support as needed by the group.

The air station was established at Tongue Point Naval Air Station on August 14, 1964, and relocated to the Warrenton-Astoria Airport on February 25, 1966. There were originally 22 officers and 104 active duty enlisted personnel; the number has greatly expanded since then.

Sikorsky HH-52A helicopters were originally based at Tongue Point and flew from the Warrenton-Astoria Airport during inclement weather. In March 1973, three Sikorsky HH-3F helicopters replaced the HH-52A helicopters at the air station. Two HU-25A Falcon jets were assigned to the air station for long-range support. Three HH-60 Jayhawk helicopters replaced the HH-3Fs in May 1995 and are still in use at the air station.

The Group maintains the base at Tongue Point, 160 housing units for enlisted personnel, an exchange located near the housing area in Astoria, and a medical/dental facility at the air station in Warrenton. The medical unit consists of a flight surgeon, dentist, and numerous corpsmen. Facilities at the air station also include a hangar, a public works building, a supply building, a morale building, a gymnasium, and a baseball diamond. Plans have been made for a barracks to be built in the future.

In an average year, group units respond to approximately 800 rescue calls, saving over 80 lives and assisting nearly 2,000 individuals. They also account for savings of over $150 million in property.

Fisheries patrols, known as "fish pats," are another part of the missions conducted in conjunction with the National Marine Fisheries Service. The patrols survey the foreign fishing activity within 200 miles of the west coast. The fish pat season usually runs from June 1 to October 31, even though the established quotas of hake, jack mackerel, and rockfish are usually filled before the season ends.

Coast Guard telephone technicians were also located at the air station. It was their responsibility to maintain independent Coast Guard telephone lines along the coast and inland as far east as the Tri-Cities in Washington. They also maintained the switchboards and eventually brought in a microwave system to replace the old landline system.

The National Motor Lifeboat School, established in 1980, and Rescue Swimmer School, which are located at Cape Disappointment, Washington, also provide training and handle search-and-rescue duties. Extensive hypothermia studies were conducted at Cape Disappointment in the 1980s. The research and in-water experiments were devised and overseen by Cdr. Alan Steinman of the US Public Health Service.

Many Coast Guard personnel have donated time to several local activities over the years, including the Thanksgiving food drive, Cub Scout Day Camp, and providing firewood for the elderly. There is a yearly open house, during which the public can see the workings of this branch of the military and tour the aircraft and hangar. In August 2010, Air Station and Group Astoria was designated Sector Columbia River.

Group/Air Station Astoria Commanding Officers:

Capt. R.L. Lawlis 1964–1966
Capt. J.T. Maher 1966–1969
Capt. J.T. Clune 1969–1971
Capt. Edward Nelson Jr. 1971–1974
Capt. R.G. Kerr 1974–1976
Capt. B.R. Shannon 1976–1979
Capt. H.J. Harris 1979–1980
Capt. D.E. Ciancaglini 1980–1983
Capt. W.C. Donnell 1983–1985
Capt. A.R. Adams 1985–1988
Capt. J.J. Hamilton 1988–1991
Capt. C.R. Leland 1991–1994
Capt. D.W. Kunkel 1994–1997
Capt. G.T. Blore 1997–2000
Capt. T.W. Sparks 2000–2003
Capt. M.P Farrell 2003–2006
Capt. P. Troedsson 2006–2009
Capt. D.E. Kaup 2009–2010

One

BEGINNING AT
TONGUE POINT

At 11:00 a.m. on August 14, 1964, the first US Coast Guard Search and Rescue base on the Oregon coast to use turbojet helicopters was commissioned. It was located at the inactive naval station at Tongue Point on the Columbia River in Astoria, Oregon. (USCG.)

An HH-52 hovers over Coxcomb Hill near the Astoria Column. The Sikorsky HH-52A single-turbine amphibious helicopter could operate in seas up to eight feet and fly at speeds up to 110 miles per hour. Coxcomb Hill has an elevation of 600 feet. The 125-foot-high column was dedicated on July 22, 1926. Fourteen scenes detailing the westward movement—and text about them—spiral up the sides of the column. A plaque at Coxcomb Hill commemorates the first Community Antenna Television System built in the United States. The system was built in 1949 and utilized the column for its antenna. (USCG.)

Two HH-52 helicopters landed for a photograph on Coxcomb Hill by the Astoria Column. These helicopters could operate 175 miles offshore, pick up five survivors, and return to base without refueling. They also had a four-foot-long rescue platform that could fold down from the door and extend over the water. (USCG.)

The primary mission of search and rescue was handled by 10 officers and 22 enlisted men with two turbojet Sikorsky HH-52A Seaguard helicopters. Each helicopter had a crew of three but could carry up to 10 people. The helicopters were flown from the Sikorsky factory at Stratford, Connecticut, to Tongue Point by pilots William Hampton, of the Sikorsky Company, and Lt. Wen Corley of the Coast Guard. The trip took five days and they arrived several weeks prior to the August 14, 1964, opening of the air station. (USCG.)

The helicopters were maintained and housed in Hangar No. 1, one of two hangars remaining at the inactive Tongue Point Naval Air Station after World War II. Lifting capacity of the HH-52A was 8,300 pounds. The helicopter weighed 5,700 pounds, leaving 2,600 pounds for fuel, crew, and payload. (USCG.)

The two pictures on this page show aerial views of Tongue Point. Tongue Point is now home to a Job Corps training facility, as well as numerous private companies; the land is leased from the Port of Astoria. Numerous piers remain on the east side of Tongue Point. (USCG.)

At Tongue Point, the Coast Guard base is located on the west side of the peninsula, along the heavily traveled Columbia River, just east of the town of Astoria. (USCG.)

Tongue Point is also the home port for a Coast Guard buoy tender. Buoys are repaired and maintained here prior to their placement as aids to navigation. The ships that place these buoys at their designated locations are called buoy tenders. (Don Nolan.)

Unlike the other Coast Guard vessels, buoy tenders are painted black and are named for plants—the black paint is in keeping with the rigorous lifestyle and missions they support. The *Mallow, Woodrush, Iris,* and *Fir* are several buoy tenders that have been stationed at Tongue Point. Two Coast Guard medium endurance cutters are located farther downriver at the city docks adjacent to Columbia Maritime Museum. (USCG.)

Among the support facilities provided at the Tongue Point base were an exchange, barbershop, and gas station, along with limited housing for some Coast Guard personnel. (Don Nolan.)

The gas station supplied both regular and premium gasoline for military personnel and their dependents. (Don Nolan.)

An exchange, which is the military version of a small retail store, opened at Tongue Point in 1968. It stocked military uniforms, personal care items, and a small supply of gift and grocery items. (Don Nolan.)

Jennie Baker, a Coast Guard civilian employee, is at the cash register in this interior photograph of the exchange. Only military personnel and their dependents were allowed access to the base's support facilities. (Don Nolan.)

As the amount of merchandise and demand increased, the exchange was moved to a larger facility on Tongue Point. Groceries were sold in one building and other items remained in the former building. During one holiday season, Toyland was opened in the exchange. A guest housing facility was also available for a short time across the highway at Emerald Heights, a former Navy housing area used during World War II. (Don Nolan.)

The barbershop provided complete grooming services to military personnel. A civilian barber was hired to run the barber shop. Because of strict military grooming standards, the barbershop was a popular place the week before standard monthly personnel inspections and awards ceremonies. (Don Nolan.)

Because the military strived to be self-supporting, numerous buildings were needed to house the various necessities for a self-contained operation. These buildings contained machine shops, mechanical repair areas, and a motor pool for maintaining government vehicles and equipment. (Don Nolan.)

Several other buildings on the base were designated for administration, personnel, public works, public affairs, supply, logistics, and a small sick bay (the military term for a facility that cares for medical and dental needs). The sick bay at Tongue Point was very small and was intended for minor injuries. Major problems were referred to the hospital or dentists in Astoria. (Don Nolan.)

Because of the rugged terrain on Tongue Point, many of the support buildings were small and scattered around the base. (Don Nolan.)

At the end of the pier is a Large Navigational Buoy (LNB). A similar one is at the Columbia Maritime Museum in Astoria. Developed in the 1970s to replace lightships, these buoys are 40 feet high and 40 feet in diameter. They are operated and monitored electronically. Their foghorns can be heard up to three miles away, and their 7,500-candlepower flashing lights can be seen up to ten miles away. (Don Nolan.)

Although the air station was moved to the Astoria-Warrenton airport in 1966, the buoy base and buoy tenders remained at Tongue Point. Buoys intended for placement in the Columbia River are still stored and maintained at the facility. Several other units of the group are also still located at Tongue Point. In this picture, some of the buoys are visible on the dock. (Don Nolan.)

In 1965, an HH-52A helicopter was dispatched to herd a group of six to eight elk back to safety. The elk had ventured from Highway 101 to Broadway in Seaside, Oregon, then around the turnaround at the end of the street, onto the beach, and into the ocean. The elk were sent back to the safety of the forest east of Seaside. (USCG.)

An HH-52A helicopter awaits a mission outside of its hangar at Tongue Point in 1964. (USCG.)

Two

WARRENTON-ASTORIA REGIONAL AIRPORT

Clatsop County Regional Airport, a former US Navy facility, became Astoria Airport and then the Warrenton-Astoria Airport. It was used for emergencies during inclement weather and for the landing of fixed-wing aircraft until the new air station was built in 1966. (USCG.)

In 1966, the new, $450,000 Coast Guard hangar was under construction at the Astoria Airport. The station would have a total complement of 10 pilots and 40 crewmen. (USCG.)

This image shows the construction of the new hangar, a single building that could hold four helicopters. The maintenance shops were on the ground floor, and the offices and watchstanders' quarters were on the second floor. (USCG.)

April 13, 1966, was the date of the official dedication of the US Coast Guard Air Station at Clatsop County Regional Airport. The ribbon was cut by Mrs. Julie Schmidtman, wife of Adm. Richard D. Schmidtman of the 13th Coast Guard District, assisted by the air station commanding officer, Cdr. Robert L. Lawlis. (USCG.)

Two HH-52A helicopters sit at the ready in the newly constructed Coast Guard hangar. The helicopters left Tongue Point at 10:15 a.m. and landed at the new complex at the Clatsop County Regional Airport at 11 a.m. (USCG.)

OFFICERS AND ENLISTED PERSONNEL

COAST GUARD AIR STATION, ASTORIA, OREGON

13 APRIL 1966

Commander Robert L. Lawlis, USCG - Commanding Officer

Lieutenant Commander Robert C. Branham, USCG - Executive Officer

LCDR R. R. Houvener, USCG
LCDR R. L. Burns, USCG
LCDR B. R. Shannon, USCG
LT J. M. Wypick, USCG
LTJG J. D. Hartman, USCG
LTJG B. F. Revert, USCGR
CHRELE R. G. Keim, USCG
CHRELE E. C. Moore III, USCG

CAUSLEY, C. M., ADCMAP-P1, USCG
BEYER, P. B., ATCP-S1, USCG
PRITCHETT, E. R., AMCP, USCG

BARNES, G. D., AE3, USCG	KINGSBURY, M. K. AM3, USCG
BARON, G. M., AD1, USCG	LEVY, L. A., PR2, USCG
BELKNAP, D. R., SN, USCG	LOOP, E. C., AE3, USCG
BIESEN, D. J., HM1, USCG	MELTON, L. A., AD3, USCG
BORGER, R. P., AT3-S1, USCG	MONAHAN, P. K., RM1, USCG
BOYD, R. C., AT2-S1, USCG	MOXLEY, D. J., AT3, USCG
CALHOUN, C. R., AD2, USCG	NEISNER, C. R., AD3, USCG
DEAN, L. W., YN2, USCG	PARENT, P. L., AE3, USCG
DORMAN, R. E., AT2-S1, USCG	PERKINS, D. A., AD2, USCG
FALLS, D. A., AD1, USCG	PERRY, C. L., AM3, USCG
FRANZEN, P. H., AE1, USCG	RACKLEY, E. C., AT1-S1, USCG
FURQUERON, J. H., AE2, USCG	SCHENK, T. L., AE3, USCG
GATLIN, W. L., SNAD-P1, USCG	SERBIN, J. R., AD1, USCG
GOODLAND, H. L., AM1, USCG	SHULTS, E. F., AD3, USCG
HAYDEN, R. W., AT3, USCG	STOREY, W. B., AM3, USCG
HOPKINS, W. H., SK1AK-P1, USCG	SUTTERLIN, J. G., AM3, USCG
HUNT, L. M., AT2-S1, USCG	WATKINS, H. A., AE3, USCG
JONES, W. L., AT2-S1, USCG	WENZEL, D. A., SNAT, USCG

Here is part of the program for the dedication of the new air station. (John Furqueron.)

24

The Warrenton-Astoria airport has had several commuter airlines over the years. There is also a Fixed Base Operator (FBO) and an aviation repair facility on the field. There is a tetrahedron that shows the direction of the wind and a compass rose painted on the field so that pilots can align their aircraft compass systems and directional gyros. (USCG.)

Lektro, a company that manufactures electric aircraft tugs, occupies the two large hangars on the left in this aerial view. The two hangars are a legacy from when the field was operated by the US Navy during World War II. (USCG.)

This aerial view shows the addition of new buildings to the air station facility. Buildings were later added to house administration, public works, medical facilities, and a gym. There are plans to eventually add a barracks and galley to the facility. (USCG.)

Cdr. Robert Lawlis transferred command of the new station to Cdr. James T. Maher on August 1, 1966. Commander Maher was transferred from Air Station San Francisco to Air Station Astoria. Cdr. Bernie Hoyland was the executive officer of the air station. (USCG.)

Cdr. James T. Maher (right) reads his orders as the new commanding officer. Standing behind him are, from left to right, Adm. Richard Schmidtman, Lt. Tony Ford, and Capt. Robert Lawlis. (USCG.)

Two HH-13N Bell helicopters—nicknamed "Snoopy" and "Red Baron"—were deployed from the air station for duty aboard the Coast Guard icebreaker *Northwind* in the Arctic. These "Bubble Bells" provided aviation support for the icebreaker. They were transported to the air station aboard a C-130 multiengine aircraft. (Capt. Jeffrey Hartman.)

Pictured with the HH-13N helicopter before deployment on the CGC *Northwind* on June 7, 1967, are, from left to right, (kneeling) AD1 George Baron, Lt. Jeffrey Hartman, AD2 Fred Todenhagen, and AT2 Bob Hayden; (standing) Lt. Ronald Addison, AE3 Harold Watkins, LCDR Dick Burns, and AE2 John Furqueron. (John Furqueron.)

The crew of the "Snoopy" included, from left to right, (first row, kneeling/squatting) AD2 Fred Todenhagen and AD1 George Baron; (second row) AE2 John Furqueron, Lt. Ronald Addison, LCDR Dick Burns, AT2 Bob Hayden, Lt. Jeff Hartman, and AE3 Harold Watkins. (John Furqueron.)

In this image, the crew gathers about the "Snoopy" on the deck of the CGC *Northwind*. Pictured are, from left to right, AE3 Harold Watkins, AD2 Fred Todenhagen, AD1 George Baron, Lt. Ronald Addison, and AE2 John Furqueron. (John Furqueron.)

From July to October 1964, the CGC *Northwind* was on Bering Sea patrol. In July and August 1967, the CGC *Northwind* was performing current and hydrographic surveys in the Bering Strait. (John Furqueron.)

The CGC *Northwind* had six Fairbanks Morse 10-cylinder diesels driving six Westinghouse DC generators, which drove three electric motors. The ship was re-engined in 1974 and 1975. Her top speed in 1967 was 13.4 knots. (John Furqueron.)

LCDR Dick Burns and Lt. Ronald Addison land the "Snoopy" aboard the icebreaker *Northwind*. Both pilots and crew were temporarily deployed from Air Station Astoria. (Capt. Jeffrey Hartman.)

Both HH-13s flew patrols over the Arctic ice fields. In addition to gathering scientific data, these patrols helped the icebreaker navigate through the pack ice by finding potential routes of least resistance or open leads not readily seen from the bridge of the ship. (John Furqueron.)

Members of the helicopter crew (from left to right) AT2 Bob Hayden, AD2 Fred Todenhagen, and AD1 George Baron relax aboard the CGC *Northwind*. (John Furqueron.)

A special patch was designed for the deployment aboard the CGC icebreaker *Northwind* and also for the US Coast Guard polar explorations. The crews wore these patches with pride, as they symbolized the time and work it took to complete the mission. (John Furqueron.)

Petty officers Fred Todenhagen (left) and John Furqueron pause for a picture aboard the CGC *Northwind*. (John Furqueron.)

Lt. Ronald C. Addison greets his wife upon the return of the HH-13N helicopter to Astoria on October 10, 1968, after a three-month deployment on the icebreaker *Northwind*. (USCG.)

Both HH-13N helicopters pictured here were housed in a specially constructed hangar aboard the *Northwind*. (Capt. Jeffrey Hartman.)

The HH-13N (Bell 47) helicopters were also used for other Coast Guard missions, including search and rescue, fisheries and wildlife patrols, and supporting the US Air Force radar stations and communications facilities. (Capt. Jeffrey Hartman.)

A group of schoolchildren get a tour of the HH-13 "Bubble Bell" inside the hangar at Coast Guard Air Station Astoria. The Coast Guard facilities have always been available for field trips for the local citizens. (USCG.)

At the time of this picture, the Commandant's Bulletin 21-86 stated that the Sikorsky HH-52A helicopter (behind the venerable Bell HH-13 in this image) had "rescued more persons from distress than any other helicopter in the world." (USCG.)

Snow and ice were occasional occurrences at the air station in Astoria. The tow vehicle moves the HH-52A by connecting to the rear wheel of the helicopter. (John Furqueron.)

An HH-52A helicopter sits outside the Astoria hangar as a fire extinguisher and a tow vehicle stand by. (USCG.)

An HU-16 Albatross, nicknamed "The Goat," was an amphibious twin-engine aircraft made by Grumman Aircraft. The aircraft was in service with the Coast Guard from May 1951 until March 10, 1983. The plane was an occasional visitor at Air Station Astoria. In 1970, the Coast Guard changed the paint scheme on their aircraft to the stripe. (USCG.)

Here, Petty Officer Bob Page works on the engine of an HH-52A helicopter. Page was an air station trophy winner for "Best Crewman" from June 1968 to January 1969. (USCG.)

CWO Ernie Moore (left) and AD1 Garry Gorst take a break in one of the shops on the main floor of the hangar. (John Furqueron.)

The crewmen who worked in the Aviation Electronics shop were responsible for the electrical equipment and avionics aboard the aircraft. Unlike today, when most electronics are simply replaced, in those days the crewmen opened the black boxes and made repairs and adjustments before returning the equipment to service. Here, AE3 Dan Knuth works in the avionics shop at Astoria Air Station. (John Furqueron.)

The crewmen in the Aviation Machinist Mate's (AD) shop were the mechanics who maintained the engines and drivetrains of the aircraft. AD1 Garry Gorst (left) and AD2 Chuck Calhoon are shown in the shop. (John Furqueron.)

In this photograph, Senior Chief Briscoe (right) receives congratulations from the 13th Coast Guard District admiral at a district inspection of personnel and the air station. (USCG.)

A Sikorsky HH-52A helicopter flies north over the Hammond mooring basin in this mid-1960s image. Construction of the Astoria-Megler Bridge, located east of Hammond, which would link Oregon and Washington, began in 1966. Portions of the movie *Free Willy* were filmed at the Hammond mooring basin. (John Furqueron.)

The bridge below this HH-52A helicopter links Warrenton to Astoria. Young's Bay is to the right and the Columbia River is to the left of the bridge. Adjacent to the vehicle bridge is the old railroad bridge, and the completed Astoria-Megler Bridge is in the background. At one time, there was an active seaplane ramp leading from the bay that allowed amphibious aircraft to access the airport. The ramp was constructed by the Navy during World War II. (USCG.)

Here, Capt. James T. Maher (at microphone) receives a commendation medal for meritorious service from Rear Adm. Frank V. Hilmer. Captain Maher retired in August 1969, and command of the air station was transferred to Capt. J.T. Clune, who had been transferred from Air Station Elizabeth City, North Carolina, to Astoria. (USCG.)

Capt. James T. Maher (top), Master Chief Clyde M. Causley, and Chief Charles Stout (lower left) prepare for their final Coast Guard flight. The three were to retire on July 31, 1969. Chief Stout served for 20 years, and Master Chief Causley retired after 28 years of service. (USCG.)

Master Chief Clyde "Crash" Causley flies at the controls of an HH-52A helicopter. Master Chief Causley was one of only a few enlisted pilots in the Coast Guard. He entered the Coast Guard on August 1, 1941, and was honored for attaining 3,000 pilot hours within helicopters. He completed helicopter training in July 1944 and was qualified in 14 types of fixed-wing aircraft and eight models of helicopters. (USCG.)

The officers and crew of Astoria Air Station are pictured with an HH-52A helicopter in July 1969. (USCG.)

Crewmen transfer an injured person from an ambulance to be transported by Coast Guard helicopter to a hospital in Portland. (USCG.)

The same patient is prepared for loading aboard the HH-52A helicopter for the flight to Portland. Medical and humanitarian transportation was often provided via Coast Guard helicopter. (USCG.)

Capt. J.T. Clune was relieved in 1971 by Cdr. Edward Nelson Jr. Here, Commander Nelson is pictured in front of an HH-52A helicopter. Commander Nelson assumed command of the air station and group on July 30, 1971. (Adm. Ed Nelson.)

Cdr. Edward Nelson Jr. (left) presents an award to an unidentified service member. Commander Nelson retired as a rear admiral and lives in Astoria, Oregon. (Adm. Ed Nelson.)

Portable buildings like the one on the left were used during renovation of the hangar to provide additional office space. An HU-16 Albatross (left) and an HH-52A helicopter are visible in this image. (Adm. Ed Nelson.)

Cdr. Edward Nelson Jr. (left) and LCDR Dave Corson inspect the engineering department personnel at the air station. (Adm. Ed Nelson.)

In this image of an awards presentation at the air station, Lt. Frank Cole is in the foreground with Lt. Miller Chappel to his right. (Adm. Ed Nelson.)

Lt. Owen Fulmer is the tall officer in the background of this group photograph from the air station awards ceremony. (Adm. Ed Nelson.)

Awards were given to Petty Officers Reynolds (left) and Kropff at a personnel inspection at the Motor Lifeboat Station Tillamook Bay, located in Garibaldi, Oregon. (Adm. Ed Nelson.)

Cdr. Edward Nelson Jr. inspects the personnel at Base Tillamook. (Adm. Ed Nelson.)

BMC Maroney and Cdr. Edward Nelson Jr. conduct an awards ceremony at Base Tillamook in Garibaldi, Oregon. (Adm. Ed Nelson.)

Chief Maroney (right) was a motor lifeboat instructor at Base Tillamook. (Adm. Ed Nelson.)

A crewman is hoisted aboard an HH-52A helicopter during a training exercise. (USCG.)

An HH-52A helicopter lands in the water to rescue a crewman during a training exercise, with a motor lifeboat in the background. (USCG.)

This picture shows an HH-52 helicopter secured to the deck of a Coast Guard cutter. (USCG.)

This HH-52A helicopter is securely chained to the rolling deck of a Coast Guard cutter to help prevent loss or damage. (John Furqueron.)

A survivor is hoisted aboard a Coast Guard helicopter after being picked up by a 44-foot Coast Guard motor lifeboat. (USCG.)

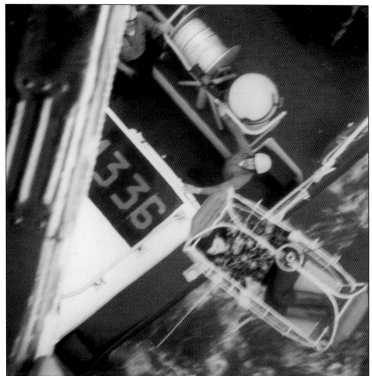

An HH-52A helicopter provides assistance by dropping a pump to a sinking fishing boat. The crew of the motor lifeboat has also secured a line on the boat. After passengers are rescued, the boat is often towed into a safe harbor. (USCG.)

AD1 Don Falls works on a General Electric T58 turbine engine. This engine was used on both the HH-3F and HH-52A helicopters. (USCG.)

HH-52A helicopter No. 1376 flies over the abandoned trestle built in the 1800s for the train that carried rock for the construction of the south jetty at the mouth of the Columbia River. (USCG.)

Two HH-3F helicopters and a C-130 sit on the tarmac at the air station. The C-130 had flown in from Air Station San Francisco. The HC-130 Hercules turboprop was built by Lockheed. The first B model entered service in the Coast Guard fleet in 1959. (John Glen.)

In March 1973, the HH-52A helicopters were replaced by three larger twin-engine Sikorsky HH-3F helicopters. The HH-3F helicopter was capable of flying 300 miles offshore, hovering for 20 minutes, picking up six people, and returning to the base. (John Glen.)

This patch was designed for the arrival of the HH-3F helicopter. The helicopter was nicknamed "The Pelican." (USCG.)

A crewman on an HH-3F helicopter photographed two other HH-3F helicopters flying in formation over the Columbia River. (Art Smith.)

The Astoria-Megler Bridge, which spans the Columbia River from Oregon to Washington, is behind the HH-3F helicopter as it flies over a 52-foot MLB out of Cape Disappointment. (Bob Ginn.)

This HH-3F helicopter is parked in the hangar for maintenance. The back ramp of the HH-3F dropped down to allow for equipment to be loaded or unloaded. (Bob Ginn.)

Capt. B.R. Shannon and his wife, Dorie, are shown at the Coast Guard Air Station after an awards ceremony. Captain Shannon took command of the air station in 1976. (Wendy Richardson.)

Fisheries patrols occurred several times each week. The HH-3F and her crew—plus an agent from the National Marine Fisheries Service—survey the area where fish are being caught to make sure all ships are abiding by regulations created by the Fishery Conservation and Management Act of 1976, which created a 200-mile American fishery conservation zone. (USCG.)

Captain B.R. Shannon greets Adm. John B. Hayes, USCG commandant, as he arrives on his Grumman Gulfstream II at the air station. Pictured are, from left to right, Elizabeth Hayes, Admiral Hayes, Cdr. Dave Andrews, Captain Shannon, Bob Gipe, unidentified, and Dorie Shannon. (USCG.)

Adm. John B. Hayes (left), Capt. B.R. Shannon (center), and Vice Adm. Charles Larkin, 13th District commander, confer on the tarmac at the air station. (USCG.)

During his visit, Adm. John B. Hayes visited many of the units in the group. Here, Admiral Hayes (left) and Rear Adm. Richard Cueroni confer aboard a self-righting surfboat. (USCG.)

Admiral Hayes and Rear Adm. Charles Larkin continue the inspection during Admiral Hayes's visit to Cape Disappointment. (USCG.)

Wet drills were held in Cullaby Lake, about five miles south of the air station. The lake is the only one in the county that allows motorized vessels; it is also used by the Clatsop County sheriff's department for drills. In training exercises, crewmen jumped into the water and were rescued by helicopters from the air station. (John Glen.)

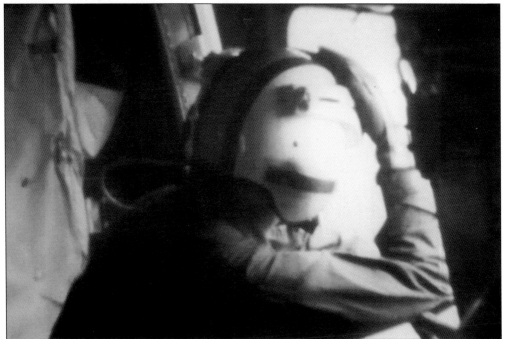

A crewman leans from the door of an HH-3F helicopter as he prepares to hoist someone up from the lake during a wet drill. (Bill Seipt.)

On May 18, 1980, Mount St. Helens erupted in Washington. Units from the Air Station Astoria responded to aid in search and rescue operations. (USCG.)

The plume from the erupting volcano could be seen from Airport Road leading into the air station in Warrenton, Oregon. Ash fell over the surrounding area even though the volcano was over 80 air miles from the station. (John Glen.)

As the eruptions continued, HH-3 helicopters from the air station continued flights to rescue trapped survivors and perform aerial reconnaissance. Trees knocked down by the volcano's blast littered the landscape and the flow raised the Tootle River and its tributaries far above flood stage, creating massive devastation. (USCG.)

The devastation caused by the flow from the volcano resulted in mass destruction. Many people and animals perished, businesses were destroyed, and homes burned. Today, there has been a renewal of the area and a national park has opened near the mountain. (USCG.)

Mission support was increased with the arrival of two HU-25A Falcon Guardian fan-jet aircraft in October 1983. A new station patch was designed for the arrival of the aircraft. (John Glen.)

The station also had a patch depicting just the HU-25A Falcon. (John Glen.)

In 1987, the HH-3F helicopters were replaced by three HH-65A Dolphin helicopters powered by LTS101-750B-2 turboshaft engines built by Textron Lycoming (now Honeywell) in Williamsport, Pennsylvania, and electronic systems manufactured by Rockwell Collins of Cedar Rapids, Iowa. (USCG.)

The HH-65 performs missions ranging from drug interdiction to polar ice patrols. It has a computerized flight management system that integrates communication and navigation equipment and allows the pilot to bring the aircraft to a stable hover 50 feet above an object. The HH-65 aircraft were painted bright orange. Although no longer at Air Station Astoria, the HH-65s are still present at other Coast Guard air stations. (USCG.)

The HH-65 Dolphin is a twin-engine helicopter manufactured by American Eurocopter (formerly Aerospatiale Helicopter Corporation) in Grand Prairie, Texas. The aircraft can be recognized by its Fenestron tail rotor. (USCG.)

The HH-65 is not capable of landing on water. It normally carries a four-person crew: pilot, co-pilot, flight mechanic, and rescue swimmer. Here, a crewman is being hoisted to the helicopter during a training exercise. (USCG.)

From 1992 until 2006, this unique patch was used by Air Station Astoria personnel. (USCG.)

The same logo was also displayed on a sign outside the air station in Warrenton. (USCG.)

On May 28, 1995, the HH-65A helicopters and the HU-25 Falcon jets were replaced with three HH-60J Jayhawk helicopters. (USCG.)

A twin-engine helicopter, the HH-60J Jayhawk carries a crew of four and can hoist an additional six people aboard. It can fly a distance of 300 miles, remain on scene for 45 minutes, and return to base with reserve fuel remaining. (USCG.)

An HU-25 Falcon, HH-65A Dolphin helicopter, and HH-60J Jayhawk helicopter fly over the air station during an open house. The HU-25 Guardian can operate from sea level to an altitude of over 42,000 feet. It has the ability to fly for five hours with a radius of 160 miles. The HU-25 was manufactured by Dassault. (John Glen.)

The crew of an HH-60 practices hoisting a crewman. (USCG.)

An HH-60J performs a hoist while three young boys watch. (USCG.)

The HH-60J flies up the Columbia River past a cutter displaying ceremonial flags. (USCG.)

With the transition to a new aircraft, a new station patch was designed. (USCG.)

The HH-60J uses the Global Positioning System as its main navigational aid and can receive information from four satellites simultaneously. Here, the aircraft is flying over the Columbia River near Portland, Oregon. (USCG.)

The HH-60J models have been in a program to upgrade avionics and capabilities to the MH-60T since 2007. All HH-60J aircraft are expected to complete this upgrade by 2015. They will then be designated MH-60T. (USCG.)

The radar in the nose gives the HH-60J a very distinctive appearance. A FLIR (forward-looking infrared) sensor turret can be mounted below the nose. (USCG.)

The pattern on the water is created by the rotor wash from the helicopter. The HH-60J has a four-blade rotor system. The rotor blades are very distinct in this night picture over water illuminated by the helicopter's hover lights. (USCG.)

Two HH-60Js await missions inside the hangar. (USCG.)

Petty Officer Easley looks out the door of the helicopter as the crew prepares to hoist the rescue swimmer aboard. (USCG.)

The rescue swimmer is hoisted up and into the helicopter. (USCG.)

This HH-60J is transporting the fuselage of a UH-1 "Huey" helicopter to be placed atop a platform. (USCG.)

This is the same HH-60 completing the Huey delivery. (USCG.)

An HH-60 flies along the beach on its return to Air Station Astoria. (USCG.)

This VTOL (vertical take-off and landing) Osprey is parked in the air station hangar. (USCG.)

This photograph shows the interior of the aircraft hangar at the air station. It has undergone many changes since it was initially constructed and has doubled in size over the years. (USCG.)

The color guard presents the colors at every important function held at the Coast Guard air station. (USCG.)

The Coast Guard are often asked to provide a color guard for community events and parades. (USCG.)

The exchange was moved from Tongue Point to its current location on Marine Drive in Astoria in 1995. Satellite exchanges like the one shown were located at the various units. (USCG.)

The exchange at the air station had very limited space and only provided snacks and essential items. (USCG.)

The new exchange is housed in the former Prairie Market. It carries limited groceries and household items, as well as uniforms and furniture. (Author's collection.)

The complex also includes a gas station for use by military members and their dependents. (Author's collection.)

Three

UNITS OF THE GROUP

There are some facilities that, although no longer active, have been an important part of the Coast Guard history at Group Astoria. The North Head Lighthouse was constructed in 1898 to mark the northern entrance to the Columbia River. It is approximately two miles south of the lighthouse at Cape Disappointment. Although the lighthouse is only 65 feet high, it sits on a bluff 130 feet above the Pacific Ocean. (USCG.)

Cape Meares Lighthouse was built in 1890 and served as the light station for Tillamook Bay. The lighthouse was deactivated in 1963. (USCG.)

In 1963, the Cape Meares light was replaced by this newer and more efficient tower. (USCG.)

Tillamook Rock Light was commissioned in 1878 and completed in January 1881. It was decommissioned in 1957. It is about 20 miles south of the Columbia River and approximately 1.5 miles offshore. It was replaced in 1957 by a whistle buoy located just west of the old lighthouse. (USCG.)

On April 11, 1892, the Columbia River Lightship LV-50 became the first active lightship on the west coast. A large navigational buoy (LNB) replaced the lightship in 1979. The lightship is now moored at the Columbia River Maritime Museum in Astoria and is open to the public for tours. (USCG.)

The lifeboat station at Point Adams in Hammond, Oregon, was built in 1889 and closed in January 1967. The building now houses the National Oceanic and Atmospheric Administration. The responsibilities of the station are handled by Coast Guard Station Cape Disappointment, which is located across the Columbia River from Point Adams. (Author's collection.)

The Point Adams Lighthouse was lit on February 15, 1875. It became redundant following the placement of the Columbia River lightship in 1892, so it was closed in 1899 and demolished in 1912. (Seaside Historical Society.)

Cape Disappointment Lighthouse was built in 1856. It was the first Coast Guard facility at the mouth of the Columbia River. The lifeboat station at Cape Disappointment was ready for service in 1879 and was manned by volunteers for the first year. (USCG.)

HH-52 helicopter 1376 flies past the North Head Lighthouse while on a routine patrol. (USCG.)

The station at Cape Disappointment is home to the Coast Guard Motor Lifeboat School, which was activated in the winter of 1968 and expanded in 1978. The first coxswain's insignia was presented to Master Chief Thomas McAdams by Commandant Admiral Chester R. Bender in 1972. (USCG.)

Pictured here are members of the Motor Lifeboat School. Chief Thomas McAdams (center) was known for smoking a cigar when the lifeboat went out on a rescue—if he spit out the cigar, it meant the boat was about to roll. The crewmen on the motor lifeboats know that if they look up and see solid water, they have two seconds to take in a lungfull of air before the boat rolls over. Although the boat will right itself, the crew will be underwater for about 30 seconds. From left to right are EN1 Larry Allen, EN1 Stan Kubo, McAdams, BMC Larry Hicks, and BM1 Bill Robinson. (USCG.)

THIS IS THE ONLY MOTOR LIFEBOAT SCHOOL IN THE WORLD, FOR OPERATING IN HEAVY SURF.

"CAN'T NEVER DID A DAMN THING, BUT TRY ALWAYS DID."

1973 MLB School Instructors

BMCM Tom McADAMS
EN1 Larry ALLEN   BMC Larry HICKS
EN1 Stan KUBO   BM1 Bill ROBINSON

In this photograph from the Motor Lifeboat School, BMC Tom McAdams is kneeling second from left in the first row. Cdr. Ed Nelson is standing at far left in the third row and Cdr. Nat Spadaford is at far right in the third row. (Adm. Ed Nelson.)

This photograph was taken at a Motor Lifeboat School graduation, with BMC Tom McAdams standing at far left and Capt. Bobby Dunn on the far right. (Adm. Ed Nelson.)

The 30-foot surf rescue boat (SRB) was introduced in 1983. It was both self-righting and self-bailing. (USCG.)

The treacherous Columbia River Bar at the mouth of the Columbia River provides an excellent area for training. The surge where the river meets the Pacific Ocean has claimed many ships, earning it the nickname "Graveyard of the Pacific." (USCG.)

At times, the motor lifeboats (MLBs) from Cape Disappointment work in tandem with helicopters, as pictured here. (USCG.)

In 1964, Cape Disappointment transitioned from the 36-foot motor lifeboat to the 44-foot motor lifeboat (MLB). This is the 36-foot MLB. (USCG.)

The 40-foot motor lifeboat served the Coast Guard for many years, and although they were much faster than the 44-foot MLBs, they were not self-righting and were restricted to operation in calmer waters. (USCG.)

The difference in size and technology can be seen in this picture of a 40-foot motor lifeboat (MLB) alongside a 52-foot MLB at Cape Disappointment. (USCG.)

The 44-foot motor lifeboat was steel-hulled, unlike its wood-hulled predecessors. (USCG.)

At Cape Disappointment, the 44-foot motor lifeboat was replaced by the new 47-foot motor lifeboat in 1996. The CG-44300, similar to the one shown here, is on display at the Columbia River Maritime Museum in Astoria, Oregon. (USCG.)

The 47-foot MLB was designed to withstand hurricane-force winds and heavy seas. If the boat were to capsize, it would self-right in less than 15 seconds with all equipment completely functional. The 47-foot MLB has a watertight survivor's compartment equipped with first-aid capabilities. (USCG.)

Sometimes during training or when working in tandem, the motor lifeboats endure extremely rough conditions. High winds and rough seas often cause the entrance to the Columbia River to be closed to all vessel traffic. (USCG.)

The 52-foot self-righting motor lifeboat *Victory* passes below the Cape Disappointment Lighthouse. (USCG.)

This image shows four 52-foot motor lifeboats, identified from left to right as 52313 *Intrepid*, 52315 *Invincible*, 52314 *Triumph II*, and 52312 *Victory*. (USCG.)

The crew aboard a 52-foot motor lifeboat takes the boat out in calm water. The large cans each contain a pump for removing water when a boat is in danger of sinking. (Bob Ginn.)

The motor lifeboat *Triumph II* replaced *Triumph I*. *Triumph I*, CG-52301, was lost on January 12, 1961, during a search-and-rescue mission for the vessel *Mermaid*. Five Coast Guard personnel and the two-person crew of the *Mermaid* were lost. (USCG.)

Rear Adm. Richard Schmidtman and other local dignitaries gather aboard the 52-foot motor lifeboat *Triumph* at Cape Disappointment. (USCG.)

The motor lifeboat 41332 rolled and sank with 10 crewmen aboard on the night of November 15, 1977, while on a training mission off Clatsop Spit. Seven of the crew were rescued before the vessel sank approximately seven miles from the entrance of the Columbia River. Three crewmen perished. (USCG.)

A 15- to 20-foot wave caught the 41332 near Buoy 14, next to Clatsop Spit, and rolled it. (USCG.)

Capt. Leo Black took the Coast Guard cutter *Iris* to sea to search for the 41332. The US Navy ship USS *Pigeon* arrived to handle the recovery. (USCG.)

The 41332 was located and hoisted from the bottom by the USS *Pigeon* (ASR-21), a deep submergence rescue vessel. (USCG.)

The Grays Harbor Lighthouse was originally known as Peterson Point when built in 1897 and commissioned in 1898. The building was given to the government services administration in 1971. (USCG.)

Grays Harbor Station is now located in the middle of the town of Westport, Washington. Note the long ramp from the boathouse in the center at the old Grays Harbor Station. The boats could be kept inside and then launched down the ramp when needed. A new lifeboat facility was dedicated in October 1973. (USCG.)

Station Willapa Bay was built in 1897. The light went into operation October 1, 1858. It was known as Cape Shoalwater Lighthouse. In 1939, the lighthouse was declared unsafe and abandoned. (USCG.)

Station Tillamook Bay was initially constructed in 1907, with a new building erected in 1946. (USCG.)

Station Tillamook Bay is located in Garibaldi, Oregon. The current station was inaugurated in 1981, and the old station was converted into a housing unit. It was placed in the National Register of Historic Places in 1994. (USCG.)

This bird's-eye view shows the entrance to Tillamook Bay. (USCG.)

Cdr. Edward Nelson Jr. (right) presents awards at Station Tillamook Bay. (Adm. Ed Nelson.)

Cdr. Edward Nelson Jr. (shaking hands on right) and an unidentified chief boatswain's mate present an award to an unidentified young petty officer. (Adm. Ed Nelson.)

The group commander would visit the units for advancements and awards, as well as unit inspections. (Adm. Ed Nelson.)

Cdr. Edward Nelson Jr. returns the salute of a petty officer second class after presenting him with an award. (Adm. Ed Nelson.)

The Coast Guard memorial at Garibaldi, Oregon, pays tribute to those who have perished in performance of their duties. The 36-foot motor lifeboat CG36513 is part of the memorial. (Author's collection.)

The Tongue Point area beyond the Coast Guard base is occupied by the Job Corps, and several industries are located in the old hangars and dock area where the air station originated. (Author's collection.)

The Coast Guard Advanced Rescue Swimmer School was established at Astoria in 1995 and is located at Tongue Point. In this image from April 9, 1996, Vice Adm. Dick Herr (center) cuts the ribbon with Capt. Bob Foley to officially open the Advanced Rescue Swimmer School. (Darell Gelakoska.)

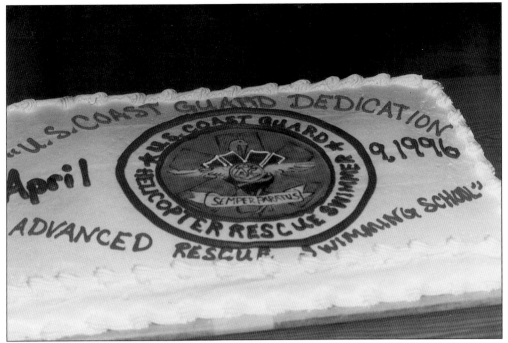

Refreshments, including this cake, were enjoyed at the dedication. (Darell Gelakoska.)

Rescue swimmers from throughout the Coast Guard attended the dedication ceremony for the new school. (Darell Gelakoska.)

Capt. Dave Kunkel (right) presents ASM2 Smith with a graduation certificate. ASM2 Smith was one of the first graduates of the Advanced Rescue Swimmer School. (Darell Gelakoska.)

Master Chief Darell Gelakoska (far left in the second row) spearheaded the establishment of the Advanced Rescue Swimmer School. He is pictured with one of the classes. (Darell Gelakoska.)

Capt. Bob Foley, commanding officer of the Aviation Training Center in Mobile, Alabama, presented Vice Adm. Dick Herr with a certificate of appreciation for his participation in the establishment of the Advanced Rescue Swimmer School. Vice Admiral Herr was instrumental in getting approval for the school from the Coast Guard. (Darell Gelakoska.)

In 1995, Capt. Dave Kunkel, commanding officer of Air Station Astoria, designated the old Coast Guard Exchange building for use as the training facility. The Coast Guard Civil Engineering Unit completely gutted the building and outfitted it with the latest audio-visual classroom equipment and locker-room facilities. (Darell Gelakoska.)

Students in the Advanced Rescue Swimmer School undergo cave and wet rock training at Cape Disappointment. (Darell Gelakoska.)

Members of the rescue swimmer team rest between training exercises. (Darell Gelakoska.)

A rescue swimmer is deployed from an HH-60J helicopter to the cliffs near North Head Lighthouse at Cape Disappointment, Washington. (Jim Sherman.)

This picture shows a rescue swimmer and survivor as they are hoisted back up to the helicopter. (Darell Gelakoska.)

A Coast Guard Aids to Navigation Team delivers a new navigational aid and fog horn to the north jetty at the entrance to Tillamook Bay. (John Glen.)

A Coast Guard HH-3F and crew prepare to longline the new aid to its assigned position on the north jetty. (John Glen.)

The LORAN (Long Range Navigation) station at Point Grenville was part of a coastal chain of stations maintained to provide an electronic aid to navigation for ships at sea. Point Grenville Station was established in June 1945 and operated by the US Coast Guard. Operations ceased in December 1979. The station was disestablished in January 1980. In this image, an HH-3F helicopter sits next to the tower at Point Grenville station. Helicopters were often used to move personnel and equipment on and off the station. (John Glen.)

The Aids to Navigation Team (ANT) is located at Tongue Point. Helicopters are used to bring members of the team to remote areas and to transport cement, batteries, and other supplies needed for their work. This helicopter is hauling a bucket of cement. (USCG.)

An HH-60J nears the area where the cement will be delivered. In order to provide safe and efficient delivery of cement to the new site, the process requires precision flying by the helicopter crew and constant communication with the Aids to Navigation Team on the ground. (USCG.)

This picture shows the Aids to Navigation Team building a new navigation marker. Navigation aids include buoys, land-based day boards, whistles, bells, and lights. (USCG.)

Aids to navigation markers assist vessels entering and leaving the waterway. Navigation aids are positioned along the entire navigational portion of the waterway. (USCG.)

This Aids to Navigation Team was brought to Lopez Island, located in the San Juan Islands off the coast of Washington. The HH-3 from Air Station Astoria supported Group Port Angeles for Aids to Navigation. (John Glen.)

When the Aids to Navigation Team stopped at Lopez Island for lunch, a car was provided by the local restaurant so the crews could get to and from the airport, which was several miles out of town. (John Glen.)

Law enforcement is another Coast Guard duty. Law enforcement classes and hands-on training were held in conjunction with Clatsop Community College and the Coast Guard cutters located in Astoria. (USCG.)

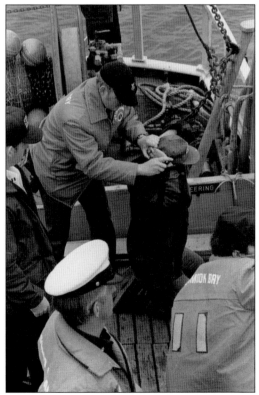

Crewmen and officers from the Coast Guard air station and small boat stations, as well as from the Coast Guard cutters stationed in Astoria, took part in the law enforcement classes. (USCG.)

The Coast Guard cutter *Yocona* was a 210-foot vessel moored at the dock near the Columbia River Maritime Museum. Pictured in a lifeboat from the *Yocona* are crewmembers taking part in a law enforcement class. Currently, the cutters *Alert* and *Steadfast* are stationed in Astoria. (John Glen.)

Boarding of vessels is often done with both the boat and the helicopter on scene and may be done either at sea or once the vessel has entered the Columbia River. (John Glen.)

Four

HOUSING

The commanding officer of the group and air station lives in housing located at Tongue Point. (Author's collection.)

In 1994 and 1995, the US Coast Guard built housing units on a hill overlooking Young's Bay. These units are occupied by families in the enlisted ranks of the service. (USCG.)

This is an aerial view of the housing area. It overlooks Young's Bay and is close to local schools. (USCG.)

Trees were cleared and streets laid out to connect to other streets in Astoria, creating a unified neighborhood. There is also a playground for children. (USCG.)

Construction of the US Coast Guard housing area started in 1994 and was completed in 1995; a total of 102 units were built. Additional land was set aside for the construction of more housing in the future. (USCG.)

There are no gates or fences to set off the area, but a sign indicates that this is government housing. After completion, the complex received a Governor's Award for excellence. (USCG.)

The unfurnished units are two-, three-, and four-bedroom and are in the style of two-story multiplexes. Occupancy is determined by the size of the family and the age and gender of the children. (USCG.)

Five

COMMUNITY INVOLVEMENT

During the month of December, Santa Claus usually arrives by helicopter and a Christmas party is held for Coast Guard members and their families in the hangar at the air station. (USCG.)

Santa Claus always has a sweet treat for the children of military personnel. On occasion, Mrs. Claus has accompanied Santa on his visit. (USCG.)

The spouses of active duty personnel have an association that is involved in many activities in the surrounding communities. Since 1980, they have held an annual Rainy Day Bazaar, usually in conjunction with the air station and Warrenton-Astoria Airport open house and air show. (USCG Spouses Organization.)

The Rainy Day Bazaar has craft booths and information booths manned by members of the community. (USCG Spouses Organization.)

The spouses' group usually sells hot dogs and a variety of baked goods to raise money for charitable organizations. (USCG Spouses Organization.)

Many civilian and military planes, in addition to aircraft from other Coast Guard facilities, arrive for the open house. (USCG Spouses Organization.)

This eye-catching display at an open house is a helicopter rescue basket. (USCG.)

On occasion, the officers at Air Station Astoria have sponsored a "dining out." This is a formal evening dinner steeped in tradition, to which spouses are invited. This November 1979 image shows a group at the Astoria Golf and Country Club, including, from left to right, Bob Ellsberg, Claudia Ellsberg, Lt. John Glen, Sue Glen, Cdr. Mikel Cole, and Sheryl Cole. (Author's collection.)

Admiral and Mrs. Wojnar and Vice Adm. Costello and others are pictured at another dining out function. (USCG Spouses Organization.)

During a Cub Scout day camp at Camp Rilea in Warrenton, Oregon, an HH-3F helicopter flew in and the young scouts were given a tour of the helicopter. Camp Rilea, an armed forces training facility on Highway 101 between Astoria and Seaside, hosts the Cub Scout day camp during the last week of June. (Author's collection.)

Easter often finds the children of personnel enjoying an Easter egg hunt and a visit from the Easter Bunny (aka the author). (Author's collection.)

This is the symbol for the Ancient Order of the Pterodactyl. The organization started in 1977 and includes all personnel who flew in Coast Guard aircraft under official orders. (John Glen.)

The Ancient Order of the Pterodactyl has held several annual reunions at the Air Station Astoria; this is a display from one of the reunions. (John Glen.)

Coast Guard aircraft fly into the Air Station Astoria carrying personnel for the Ancient Order of the Pterodactyl reunion. (John Glen.)

The Coast Guard Barque *Eagle* has visited Astoria on at least two occasions. The present-day *Eagle* was built at the Blohm & Voss Shipyard in Hamburg, Germany, in 1936, and commissioned as a training vessel for Germans. It was one of three sail-training ships operated by the pre–World War II German Navy. At the close of the war, the ship was taken as a war prize by the United States, re-commissioned as the US Coast Guard Barque *Eagle*, and sailed to New London, Connecticut, which has been its homeport ever since. (John Glen.)

In August 2010, Air Station and Group Astoria became Sector Columbia River, and a new patch was designed to identify the change. The missions of the sector include: captain of the port, marine safety, vessel inspection, search and rescue, ports waterways and coastal security, law enforcement, aids to navigation support, environmental protection, and support for units in the area. The additional units of the marine safety unit in Portland, USCG cutter *Bluebell*, and Station Portland have been added. The area covered has been extended to the Salmon and Snake Rivers in the east (Idaho) and down the Columbia River to the Oregon coast. (USCG.)

DISCOVER THOUSANDS OF LOCAL HISTORY BOOKS
FEATURING MILLIONS OF VINTAGE IMAGES

Arcadia Publishing, the leading local history publisher in the United States, is committed to making history accessible and meaningful through publishing books that celebrate and preserve the heritage of America's people and places.

Find more books like this at
www.arcadiapublishing.com

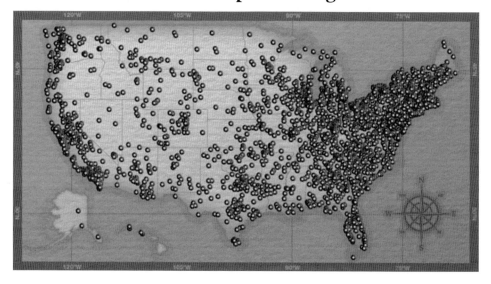

Search for your hometown history, your old stomping grounds, and even your favorite sports team.

Consistent with our mission to preserve history on a local level, this book was printed in South Carolina on American-made paper and manufactured entirely in the United States. Products carrying the accredited Forest Stewardship Council (FSC) label are printed on 100 percent FSC-certified paper.

MADE IN THE USA